Flowers

By

Steffi Cavell-Clarke

©2017
Book Life
King's Lynn
Norfolk PE30 4LS

ISBN: 978-1-78637-147-8

All rights reserved
Printed in Malaysia

Written by:
Steffi Cavell-Clarke

Edited by:
Charlie Ogden

Designed by:
Danielle Jones

A catalogue record for this book
is available from the British Library

PHOTO CREDITS

Flowers

CONTENTS

Words that look like **this** can be found in the glossary on page 24.

What Is a Plant?

A plant is a living thing. All living things need water, air and sunlight to live.

There are many different kinds of plant. Most plants have roots, leaves, flowers and a stem.

Plants live all around the world!

What Is a Flower?

A flower is a part of a plant that grows from the stem and the shoots.

Flowers have many important jobs to do. They make pollen and seeds, which are needed in order to make new plants.

What Do **Flowers** Look Like?

Sunflower

Rose

Tulip

Daffodil

Flowers come in many different shapes and sizes.

Flowers are often bright and colourful. They usually have a sweet smell too. This helps them to **attract** insects.

*Bees like the smell of **nectar**, which can be found in flowers.*

9

How Do **Flowers** Grow?

Most plants grow one or more flower heads. In order to grow, the flower heads need water, air and sunlight.

A flower starts as a small bud that grows from the shoot or the stem of a plant. When it is fully grown, the bud will open up into a flower.

Flower

Flower Bud

Parts of a Flower

Flowers have lots of different parts. Most flowers have petals and stamens. The petals help to **protect** the other parts of the flower.

In the centre of a flower are the stamens and the stigma. The stamens make the pollen.

Stigma

Stamen

13

What Do Flowers Do?

Butterflies are attracted colourful petals.

A flower's job is to attract insects and other animals using its bright colours and sweet smells.

Insects and other animals feed on the nectar that flowers make.

This butterfly is drinking nectar from a flower.

When an insect visits a flower to drink its nectar, the flower's pollen sticks to its body.

The pollen then falls off on the next flower that the insect visits.

This bee has pollen stuck to its body.

Once a flower has taken in pollen from another flower, it can make seeds.

18

Some seeds are blown away by the wind and become buried in soil. Once they have enough water and sunlight, the seeds will grow into new plants.

Flowers in the Garden

A gardener can water plants to help its flowers to grow.

Many people like to grow flowers in their gardens.

There are also lots of flowers that grow on their own. These are called wild flowers. Daffodils, bluebells and daisies are often found growing in the wild.

21

Strange Flowers

Rafflesia Arnoldii

Not all flowers smell nice. The Rafflesia arnoldii is the largest flower on Earth. It smells like rotting meat to attract flies!

The black bat flower has black petals that make it look like a bat!

Black Bat Flower

GLOSSARY

attract make something come closer
grows naturally develops and increases in size
nectar a sweet liquid found in flowers
pollen a powder-like substance made by flowers
protect look after and keep safe
soil the upper layer of earth where plants grow
sunlight light from the sun

INDEX